Closer to Home

Derk Wynand

Brick Books

CANADIAN CATALOGUING IN PUBLICATION DATA

Wynand, Derk, 1944-
Closer to home

Poems.
ISBN 0-919626-94-7

I. Title.

PS8595.Y58C56 1997   C811'.54   C97-932342-8
PR9199.3.W96C56 1997

We acknowledge the support of the Canada Council for the Arts for
our publishing programme. The support of the Ontario Arts
Council is also gratefully acknowledged.

The cover is after a painting by Eva Wynand,
'Anemones', acrylic on canvas, 78×72 cm., 1995.
Cover art photographed by Francis Sullivan.
The author photograph is courtesy of Stephen Stamp.

Typeset in Ehrhardt.
The stock is acid-free Zephyr Antique laid.
Printed and bound by The Porcupine's Quill Inc.

Brick Books
431 Boler Road, Box 20081
London, Ontario, N6K 4G6

1 2 3 4 · 99 98 97

For Eva and our parents, who define it

Contents

I.

Aerial Photograph

There's the village where we live, surrounded
by green fields never so perfectly green
at field-level when we pick our way through
spring, summer, fall. There's the roof of our house,
patched and holding up for another day,
and the welcome mat still saying welcome,
seasonal mud taking nothing away
from the greeting, though judging by the light
and the absence of traffic, I would guess
we must be (must have been) in bed, resting,
let's say, from our work through the fields of corn,
sugar beets, maybe potatoes, it's hard
to tell with these overly perfect greens,
in no mood, let's be honest, to receive
guests, not our neighbours, not our closest friends,
not even the pilots, navigators,
or the agents who hire them to haul us
out of the sheets whenever it suits them,
first to expose us, then to make us pay.

Decent Neighbourhood

A dog barks all night, small lapdog by the sound
of it, maybe with no lap to sleep on, its bark
much bigger than its bite, we imagine, never
having been bitten by it, or is it him, voice
amplified by the nearly total quiet it breaks
and breaks yet again? By day, when it's free and fed,
the dog runs among the abundant rhododendrons,
a silly pink ribbon on its head, no reason to think
it means one thing or another, though many no doubt
do wonder. Like our neighbours, we spend too much
of the night looking out the window, hollering,
thinking slaughter. The fines for cruelty especially
to animals, even tiny ones with oversized voices,
in this would-be-old-country city would strain
our wallets, not just our nerves. For once, though,
the neighbourhood appears to be standing together
on something, at last having found a clear focus
for its normally diffuse hatreds. What a shame
to waste it on such a pathetic creature whose owners
seem to have packed their bags furtively and gone,
as if they'd discovered dangerous undercurrents here
and left their dog alone in them to swim or to drown.

Night Rain

A rapping on the roof: claws or feet
clack in the attic, an odd regularity
of skeletons in closets, rats
or mice chewing the insulation off
live wires strung inside walls.
Perhaps imagined creatures are making
real connections. With tooth or beak
they tap into consciousness, pick
the wound of memory, get down to bone.
That what their noise suggests
may not exist does nothing to reassure:
one fear still generates the next
as certainly as a cloud does rain:
drop by drop the torture continues,
against metal gutter or cedar shake,
harder and harder against the skull.
The mind, at first resisting
what suggests itself, slowly begins
to provide openings, gives in.

Mowing the Lawn and Putting it Off

1. The grass, only last week straw,
    this week too lush again to cut.

    Cut anyway, wet around the blades
    and a green glue, electric motor blue,
    smoking.

    Over and over till winter, then over.

    Greener in December, not growing,
    because of these accidents of latitude
    and longitude, our city every third
    winter white.

    In the wet of it, dry enough
    by a fire, we plan to take this engine
    apart, rewire it, make it go.

2. Starlings, those European imports, but good
   for nothing, chatter on the telephone
   poles, branches, slackening lines,

   each year refusing harder to leave.

3. Taking turns, we have no better science
   for this, not quite pattern that forces us
   through ever tighter green circles.

   Our neighbour sucks in his paunch,
   round and round the green,
   his face with every turn redder.

   We cannot, cannot be like him.

   We must be, as stable now
   that the electrons in our heads
   are spinning clockwise like his.

One Version of Love

Tablecloths of the second-best Irish linen
and what looks like the silk of parachutes
have been tacked to all our neighbours' windows
except the one with its Japanese sunburst:

what wars have been fought all these years
behind them without our knowing?

One perception immediate on another sounds
more like an ordinary life than a structure,
but we keep our eyes and ears open.

Letters that need to be written
have not been written. All the creditors
and friends have not pressed hard enough.

Lately, nothing but the simple gets done
and the rewards do not last long.

We waste too much time reconstructing
bad dreams in painstaking detail,
as though they proved how crazy we were
or could be. We call nothing nightmare.

If the writing came easy as that!

Often, you think me grandiose, though I approach
you on my knees. You never tell me
what's roused your suspicions.

Often, my rage has no purpose,
though it's seldom without effect.

Behind the tablecloths, parachutes, and the flag
of the emperor, the shadows of our neighbours
make their move. They bluster and strut.
Just for us?

So night has fallen again, all
the house lights around us full up.

We concentrate on the shadows, thinking
maybe of Narcissus, increasingly paralytic,
barely able to utter his lie of an active love,
eager to believe the lie.

Keeping Up Appearances

Winter apples dotted trees without leaves,
a mist slowly washing the black branches
and fruit away, as in Chinese landscapes,
hints of more solid mountains here and there
in the background poking through, a traveller
or two perhaps in a straw hat, neither
tea- nor wine-house close by, nor bordello,
or was I confusing cultures again,
and it seemed important that the mist was
not so pure as it had appeared at dawn,
that the autumn fires outside had been
giving up their smoke all day, offering
at the same time a simple solution
to the mystery of the missing leaves,
while the neighbours, in front of wood fires,
a little drunk on medicinal wine,
grappled with questions no less difficult
to answer, exhausted too from working
all day long to hold the apples steady
in the wisps of the trees, even as smoke
and mist worked to break our concentration
that kept the fruit solid, its colours true.

Green Zone

outdoor benches chewed up
over decades by lovers with a need
to prove something

knives hauled out of pockets
after long tussling long whispering
of proper names or improper

the lovers startled out of dreams
of perfection into mundane excuses
and corrective woodwork

new initials carved into old
leaving less and less wood to support
the idea of benches

on which thoughts rain down
night and day more a brushing
of the skin than a rain

lashes aflutter at the cheek
butterfly kisses but
with real butterflies

not only the wood exposed the blood
pressing against all its vessels
giving rise to still more ideas

pushing them closer and closer
to the nervous skin
the surface again

Float Plane

The float plane groans and groans across the water and does not let go a long time. Finally, pontoons drooping in the visible heat, it cuts loose. In every mouth of those who are watching, the air dissolves into its atoms. The last snow on distant mountains turns directly to a vapour that lends its waves to the air. The mountains themselves begin to sag, deeper and deeper, so deep the gulls begin to lose all sense of direction. Fleshy clams they drop refuse to break open on soft rocks below, and hardly bounce, everything sticking to everything else now in this heat, groaning, and not even the exhibitionists willing to moan here with convincing pleasure in their voices. The saxophonist on the point's less hampered: for miles around he keeps things swinging – rocks, waves, the too buoyant light. Crabs reel out from beneath bearded logs and stones; they too would gladly step out of their clothes if they could. One crimson bikini in particular burns with the fiercest flame – the saxophonist blasts it out again, hotter, a lesson in jazz or jet propulsion. The sun inside its rainbow, in its halo of darker light, saucers off and away very happy.

On this 12th of May, 1985

all the poets of Victoria,
except those too old or too wise, have gone home
to mother.
Winter has finally released them.
The wind
never stops.
A saxophonist at the foot of the cliff
plays a wistful tune and thinks, surely, about his mother
far away on the mainland and the ferry so expensive.

He does not want to pawn his saxophone; he does not want
to play wistful tunes on the streets of the city for money.

[In time, every word and image of this poem and others
written by Victorians will have something to do
with Mother's Day, 1985.]
The mountains across the strait
look cool enough beneath their snow-caps.
The clouds lend them
a certain tone also of wistfulness and nostalgia
that the saxophonist may have missed in his playing.

The children out dragging their mothers along have all put on
ceremonial faces.
They look as though they'd rather be flying
kites their fathers have made them or cursing with their friends
like the fishwives that really do exist, even in Victoria,
not that anyone should pretend to know what children are thinking.

The sign says STAY OFF THE CLIFFS DURING WINTER MONTHS.

Winter has, as already suggested, finally let go, even if
the signs have not.
          The cliffs do not seem much more stable
now that May has arrived, nor do the words that cannot begin
to describe them as they truly are.
                              It's Mother's Day,
that's for sure and, while I'm not about to pretend
that I've lived in Victoria long enough to read the thoughts
of mountains, I can see them shimmering in the tricky air.

Who, then, could deny me their contemplation of the enormous
energies and desires that once heaved them high into being?

Angel in the House and Out

Sheets weigh down the clothesline and the holly bushes
in their back yard, rugs lie face-down in snow, ready
for beating. In these conditions, they will never
dry or be free of dust. Snow begins to cover
strung shirts and blouses, more intimate whites that sag
and sag into wintry calm, no protection now
against the elements. If she listens, she can
almost hear the flakes pile up, layer by layer,
absorbing the bad sound of things, and almost feel
the wet cloth stiffen to ice. Less audible now:
his noisy theories about shoes and old women
who live in them, his thin jokes about feet and gloves
and hands too much in them. As he struggles to come
up with more circumlocutions, she finds a way
to ignore them: she applies polish she washes
she cooks she thinks. She turns her eyes to the window.
Snow keeps falling on diapers and socks. It falls wet
and soft as snow, and soon she links it to the way
one of them pretends to listen while the other
pretends to speak. Staring at the clothesline, she sees
the creature on its back beneath, flapping its arms
in woollen layers laughing or crying, waving,
ambiguous, its calls snow-muted, bearable.

Strata

Wild sweet peas roll up the cliff, undulant
flowers, and waves of real water close in
behind, in the particulate light.

The logs on them settle ashore.

For a while longer, the limestone and sand
do not fall in on themselves.

Further along, the earth is held together
by broom, those who stop to admire it,
by something else entirely,
its blossoms without name or colour.

Those branches grow ever closer to and into
the head, thicker – a whole lifetime.

The ramifications are nothing if not considered.

If it buzzes, it's likely a bee, and no one here
to hang on to his bonnet.

Knots of kelp toss in the surf, the green cut
from the brown and reduced to nothing
but order.

Behind it: waves the eye can never quite follow
to the end, atmospheric layers that could pass
for a horizon, all of it

held firmly in place by some witness
who finds the construction good.

Seascape with Donkey

Horsetails in the air,
on the water:
roostertails.

And no horses.
And no roosters.

Somewhere must be
the tail of a donkey,
and a tailless donkey
pinned to a wall,
two-dimensional.

Imagine: a real likeness
of a donkey, real pins,
a solid wall.

Anything can be pinned to it:

an oyster-catcher, whistling,
that flies into fog
and is gone

or a freighter that blows
its own horn and slides
out of this world

or the brain itself grasping
these details, holding on.

How one part connects
with another
or fails to connect.

Maybe I'm the donkey
always needing to be
reattached to the same two
or three things on the earth
or the air or the water.

Stormy Night

On the street, three in the morning, roughly,
a driver shifts down without double-clutching,
grinds into low gear for his own amusement:
almost enough to wake the dead. The city hums.
Wind. Then more wind, gusts from the west:
on them, a dog howls, howls again, distant.
It can be pictured as some cocker spaniel pup
or beagle, maybe, the runt of the litter for sure.
How can the wind itself be pictured? German
shepherd? Dobermann pinscher, all the force
of its body concentrated on the points
of the teeth: impossible to imagine that pressure.
Wind in the various branches in the window
shakes them variously, shakes the stuff off them:
petal, last winter's leaf, berry or twig.
New and old nests ride out the storm, which the eye
does not tire of tonight, all the soft flotsam
backlit by a streetlight beyond the field
of vision, or by some other light. Everything spills
in time into the window frame and the eye remains
fixed by whatever it's attached to. It's hard
to imagine the birds on those branches asleep.
The tail, we assume, of some neighbour's cat
(we *assume* cat!) taps against the door.
By the time the porch light can expose it
for what it is and was, the animal has vanished
into night again. All cats, at night, etcetera
(and whatever else we care to assume.) Something
in sleep grinds a large axe. The dog whimpers,

or the wind, as if after remembered prey in dreams,
the furious legs not touching solid ground,
jaw slack as the tongue to allow the hot breath
to issue freely from the sleeping maw. The bodies
in the cemetery across the street do not turn
in their graves, fact that offers no consolation.
The kids we just were have begun kicking down
the headstones, pinning the serious carnations
into their buttonholes, and dancing without joy
over the freshly dug soil. They make love
less often than we like to think and, later,
have their own reasons for not sleeping.

In Autumn

Abruptly in autumn, the neighbour's house
grows visible through the alders, closer,
his lights approaching as we too prepare
for sleep. We watch him by day rake his share
of the leaves, taking care not to remark
on their gold. Damn all the clichés, we think,
full speed ahead as we work. We complain
about the weather, the work, the growing
toll on shoulder and spine, all too subject
to cold. Are we old now as our parents
were when they played those awful recordings
we so hated, by Williams, was it, and
Conniff? Jangling piano, saccharine
strings. Such stuff can prove treacherous, appear
all at once melodious – can too much
raking really soften the brain? Unmoved
by our concerns, children out of nowhere
begin to shrill, leaping headlong into
the heaped leaves until our neighbour hollers
for them to stop, shouting: Thoughtless. Feeling
nothing too precisely, we echo his cries.

A Deal We Could Live With

and though no one suggested it, they threw in
the kitchen sink for good measure, the hammock,
the smoke coil and mosquito-proof netting,
the collection of Botticelli prints – or was it
only the promise of even more breathless descriptions
of the back of her knee? They said, Take the surfboard,
the surf, the spindrift on otherwise quiet nights,
spoondrift, the sound of one or the other,
whichever you prefer, or both, the arabesques
on the hand-mirror held in her hand whenever she looks
for something she's not sure of – Venus in the foam
– whatever her own eye is window to,
reflected light, some lucky gnat blinked in.
In the distance, what must have been sunlight
bounced off the chrome fittings or glass of a boat
in distress, its paler electric light and horn
spelling out the novice captain's idea of Mayday
or SOS. Take it, too, they said, if you want,
the boat, the light, the horn, the SOS. Take the sun
beneath which she often lies tanning, and the whitecaps,
and the captain's wife not trembling below deck,
holding her fear in, saying nothing to alarm
her two children. We assume, they said,
you would have no use for a man who'd allow matters
to get so out of hand. We agreed, not blaming him
especially, but distracted by the inevitable thoughts
of our tenuous hold on everything. Maybe that's why
we could not help but conjure up the woman coming
ashore, hair and hips swinging as we followed her,

her dress foaming high to expose her legs, spindrift,
substance we could more willingly drown in,
and her daughters as beautiful, almost adults,
but sticking close to her, unaware of the close call
they had had, the dangers still ahead, and we nodded
nodded, perhaps too eager, saying, Done!

Good-byes

1. Around the house rise trumpet flowers into which overstuffed black bees disappear. This puts no end to the orange music that keeps the house a going concern, making a link between us outside and all the others inside, listening too. What good-byes have already been said go ignored now, the heavy black bodies of the insects inching closer to the source of all welcome, yellow dust, note still to be delivered to the wide world and sustained. Greetings, greetings, apple and pear tree, lazy buzz we all take comfort in, none of us budging for fear of disrupting the tune.

One bee, half-dead on the tiles yesterday, today is consumed by the ants. Before you can see, I kick its husk into the bed of foxgloves, into the tangle of stems, to keep the ants and their necessary work at a distance. Despite this, some of them – invisible – crawl up our sleeves. Swatting at them, we imagine them already into our hair and deeper.

The dead bee still vibrates, black among the flowers. Stupid ... the stupid ants.

2. Close-up, the march of ants looks more random than the straight line seen from a distance suggests. Any of them the eye stays with circles and forges ahead, back again, into and out of a rock's shelter, into trials and errors. Somehow, they progress.

Now it is flesh, now water that draws them: a dead field rat, its head already not much more than a puzzle of bones, or the bath in which you will soon try to dissolve this image without success. Ants keep swarming into centres of black activity on the terrace, carcass of bee or dragonfly or rat, more a coming than a going, the black increasing, filling in.

Of course, it's impossible. When I point the ants' behaviour out to you, you complain that it's not at all what you needed to see or know. What *that* might be, however, you do not mention. In the time I need to worry about it, the ants will have picked everything clean.

II.

The Sign of Our Prosperity

A train jumps the tracks and roars on,
through the chain-link fence and concrete
barriers at the station, past the line
of disappointed would-be passengers waving
tickets and day-passes, through the red
lights and the green lights that make no
difference to the snarled rush-hour traffic,
up one-way streets and down one-way streets
downtown and metallic through the pedestrian
zones, where nimble executives, not to be
denied, jump on, managers, politicians with
visions, stockbrokers, literary and cinematic
agents, avant-garde poets clutching their
alphabetized lunches and numerical files
in leather briefcases, and charges through
the suburbs, where inventors stop tinkering
in the basement and teenagers in the attic
abandon computer programmes that will make
them rich, and they throw open the curtains
for the first time since their housewarming
parties to let the full wonder of the train
rattle in: engine, engine, grain car, grain
car, grain car, et cetera, coal, more coal –
Jesus, what a country! – liquefied gas,
plywood, flakeboard, raw pulp, raw pulp,
raw lumber, uncut logs, logs again – raw,
etc. cornflakes and *Newsweek* and lottery
tickets, caboose, the engineer in front
in his pinstripes, delirious for joy, the

brakeman hanging on, delirious for worry,
scanning the want ads, page after page –
Jesus, etc., he's not alone, is he? – the
train breaking through, faster and faster,
slowing down for none but the few who believe
with an unshakeable conviction, visionaries,
leaving the rest of us behind, waiting to
see, waiting to see, seeing – Jesus! – then
making plans for the next train, which will
be longer, you bet, faster, yessir, just
as real, of course, and right on schedule.

Head

Eventually, we managed to eliminate
all clutter, the Mozart inflating
our small talk or vice versa,
the wallpaper that came with the house
when we bought it, snowberries choking
the arbutus outside, spent petals sticking
to the rhododendrons, ads in the paper
and most of the items advising us how
to eat better, exercise more, spend less,
buy smarter – everything but the one story
about the murdered woman's head found
by her estranged husband in a culvert
outside her home, just the plain text
about her head in the ditch he was cleaning
that day, ridding it of whatever
the local kids had tossed in, candy
wrappers, cigarette packaging, comic books, safes,
freeing it of weeds, brambles, all the nameless
growth, so that the pure
terror of his wife's head might manifest
itself there, without the distraction
of their lives to interfere,
so far without motives, without
the tidy balances of action
and reaction, cause and effect,
passion and still more passion –
just the head, freed of reason
and human or natural law,
the very idea of a head tossed
into a ditch and then found.

A Dream of Dollars Maybe

Untroubled by privilege, a service job, UI,
or the official chagrin, he sleeps at the entrance
to a federal building that no one wishes to leave,
once having entered it. Something, a dream of dollars
maybe, or nightmare, sets his hand in motion. More bone
than flesh, it's hoist into the private space of public
servants and petitioners who would step over him
and withdraws again, empty. The hand then seems to fall
asleep again, like the body, the better to dream
its single recurring dream. Beneath their lids, the eyes
remain fixed on an idea for which the head has found
plenty of time and made some room. Soot covers his face,
the exposed neck, ankles, wrists, grime of a week's lying
or sitting still. Or can these legs march? The officials
who hang, half-curious, out of windows from the top
to the ground floor make half-hearted efforts to come up
with the least offensive answer to this innocent
question. Their collective gaze ventures time and again
from the hope-filled graphs on their walls to the hand that breaks
the steadily rising curves, that thrusts, is thrust, into
lower, inner space. They note again its fingers curled,
the thumb across, making a kind of slot into which
could be dropped the smaller coins burning through their pockets
and so make the whole mechanism run, force its eyes
open, have it look at the real world, bend its spine, make
it say Thank you, grateful for such enlightenment.

Subject

From your shadow behind his shadow
behind the bushes, keep an eye on him,
novice photographer, veteran of playgrounds,
of the Battle of Britain, so the paper says,
twice-decorated Spitfire pilot,
teacher, it says, in the post-war decades,
what subject the paper did not say,
but think history, which leaves room
for invention, interpretation,
or personal development, which allows for,
even invites, the darker fantasies,
write him down for the record, photograph him,
gather the necessary proofs and do not pretend
to love him or despise him,
but only wait for him to reveal himself
at his strongest or weakest
in the not too deep forest,
in the deceptive underbrush, killing time
on the edge of a playground
reserved for children under 12,
no dogs allowed, nor old men trying to recapture
what they could never put into words,
no one ever there to enforce the restriction,
to interpret the ban to dogs or men,
and as usual, expect the worst,
all those possibilities that someone in baggy trousers
in a park or playground can suggest,
but pin no specific idea to it,
keep your mind open to everything,
don't let him see you while you observe

his barely moving head, intent on the swings
burdened with legs and skirts that fly, generously,
photograph him, if you can, as he zooms in
with his own camera, capturing the large glimpses,
or his hand in his pocket, flesh
of his bare old arm wobbling, frantic,
some boy-child or girl-child in his sights,
if obscured a little by the brush and unaware of him,
child in the clouds toward which he jerks,
pulling it down, closer to the idea of some woman
he may have made of it, pretending it's love,
caught up in his own best lie
your photos can later expose,
but do not forgive him everything, nor forget it,
because of the battles he's fought,
his age, all the habits that a war
he did not start forced him to learn,
the excuse of death always handy,
dropping suddenly out of sun or cloud
and catching the unsuspecting from behind,
novice fallen out of formation, or child,
staying on his tail and, with a shout of fear
and joy, closing in, the hero again.

My Narcissus

kneels dead centre of what he considers
the only circle

keeps one eye on the immediate foreground
the other on where he guesses
the circumference might lie

bows and bows in all the directions

presses a finger to his pulse
and takes it for hours

closes his eyes the better to enjoy
the satisfactory beating of his heart

hears a bee or a wasp fly into the circle
and threaten to sting or the bird
that means someone will die

feels then his pulse quicken unsure
whether this makes it stronger or weaker

ignores the wasp for the pulse

ignores the bird and those others
who will die

remembers Echo her heart racing
birdlike racing his heart and winning
beautiful beautiful

The Longer I Sit Here

on this very archetypal park bench
(though in nothing like the park
you must be thinking of)

the colder I get (in the familiar
shirtsleeves and the sun in a panic
flaring its nostrils, already as high
as it's likely to get)

and maybe that's why I'm shaking,
shaking (oh, you'll see or hear much
of this word from me from here on
and if you've paid attention to the world
for at least forty years you'll know
just what I'm talking about)

and the sun's really galloping now,
racing out of control high overhead
and then just ahead, and neither you
(if you've taken my meaning) nor me
calm enough or collected enough
to lunge for and pull in the reins.

Circe

... as though she had needs of her own.

... the traffic wedged to a halt along the beach, pedestrians undoing more and more straps and buttons.

... one traveller in particular talking on the third day of his visit, despite his best intentions to keep silent for a full two weeks, surprised that no one frowns at his failure.

... not that the details remain insignificant, but that they may add up to some totally unpredicted meaning.

... the pigs we all are, pigs we have been.

... after all the unsubtle approaches, his visible attempts to make eye-contact, his stuttered lines to tempt her into conversation, and her refusal to claim victory from her own constant refusals.

... she, at the end, still not victorious, but not defeated either as she bellies down into the hot sand, her breasts flat and without milk or sensations.

... pressure, the pressure and release, as in steam in an espresso machine, as in the digestive system, as in wine or in beer.

... a nation of illiterates through which an educated man travels, reading his own or others' works, thinking about sex in new ways and recording the same old thoughts, each time resorting to the same language, the moon always revolving around the same earth and everything that implies.

... as in hunger.

... as in hunger and everything that implies, and a man with a sack of grain travelling through the land, offering good prices, or a credit card and a line of credit that would make even the bank clerks pay attention.

... or what they make of one another, he speaking his language, she speaking hers, their eyes equally bloodshot, but for different reasons.

... her preference for the vegetal, his for the animal, both worlds made possible by the sun, a fact that hurts and sustains them.

... everyone paying little attention, paying something else, as tourists do, the details in time looking after themselves.

... the questions raised by these girls – girls? young women? – staking claims to their part of the beach, wearing all their gold.

... pot-bellied child?

... the girls, still girls, pretending it makes no difference who looks and who pays.

Penelope's Dream

… having lost all the names and so
adrift, saying, *Water, water, water,*
its surface not opening up
for even a second, and the sirens
on nearby rocks a memory not sharp enough
to cling to, so you drift, singing the same
two or three songs over and over,
thinking *What keeps me here?*
mulling over the paradox of being
(*being kept*) adrift and having no idea
whom or whether to blame or to praise.

One Arsonist, Two Firemen

Dog days:
>   the dogs alone bother
to make needless movements, chasing
one another among the bodies
where they lie tanning.
>   The flies
have gone into hiding.
>   A thin dream
of wind rattles the palm fronds.

To the north of us, real pine cones
crackle:
>   a pine forest goes up
in a smoke that cuts short the day.

The cloud thickens, soon lets go
its ash, like snow, without the strict
geometry of snow.
>   These flakes appear
to us as pine needles without body,
as bits of cones or feathers
of unknown birds, the fur of God
knows what animal, shreds of cloth,
now a silk that falls apart too
soon in our hands, without
joy, more grey silk then, paper
on which the words have not faded
completely.
>   Later, we think of them
as letters, written in light the fire

casts against its own cloud:

                              a note
quickly jotted by a fireman new
at this kind of love, or by a poor man
to a woman he wants dressed in silk,
a man who could profit from the fire.

Our dream, like the fire contained in it,
opens up for the firemen, the next day
found arm in arm, lovers.

                    When we awake,
their locked arms have already been broken
to separate them.

When We Grew Up

Everything had its head in the clouds
that day: the woman in her third month,
the adolescent writing his first poem,
already saying 'everything' too often,
the coed with more than one secret
she'd have been only too happy to tell,
the young highjumper about to reach
new heights, though not as he wanted,
his friends, who found themselves
inside a poem the first and only time,
many of them never to stray so far
from their homes again, the pine tree
beneath which nimbus clouds had been
summoned, the moss and pine needles
stuck in fabric, the hard cones,
the houses in which everyone slept
or tossed all night, unable to sleep,
head in the clouds and still unable
to sleep, the chimneys, the TV antennas,
the actors declaiming in the black-
and-white night owl movie, the night owl –
all with their heads in the clouds:
the cigarette, the coffee, the burned toast,
the diary with its brass lock, the wallet
with its two colour photos of one person,
the body with its body in cloudy fluid –
all their heads in the clouds that day,
the day itself with its head right in,
and the clouds still bunching up thicker.

At Two in the Morning, Say

he said, Guardian angel, fallen
asleep on the job again.

Angel, she said, drawing out
the first syllable and closing
her eyes, the smile he loved
and hated reappearing on her face.

There you go again, he said, there,
meaning nothing more specific
than away, but wanting to go along
and getting nowhere. Where
has he taken you this time?

Dancing, she said, dancing:
the ceiling won't stop spinning.

Fallen asleep again, he said.
He said, Dancing!

The smile he hated and loved
he still hated and loved.

Sleep in your clothes, then,
he said, dance away in your clothes,
stepping out of his own,
climbing into bed.

The guardian angel maybe pulled
up the covers, pulling them along,
holding his tongue,
she sleepwalking after, he keeping
in step, almost awake, neither
any longer in serious danger
of falling or being fallen upon.

Long Weekend

By Monday, the calls were repeating themselves,
the dogs outside howling for one another
or their owners and finding no answer,
grownups barking their names, while children
with nothing much to say, shouted it, testing
their voices, more than passing the test,
and an autumn gale summoned the dry leaves back
to their source, wooden matches flaring
across denim or nail to make their appeals
to kindling or straw, and inside, the telephone rang
a long time before I made up my mind to answer,
to work on perfecting our familiar arguments
over how long the distance had become,
each echo on the line another irrefutable proof,
each long split-second delay, our voices
bouncing off the moon or some other satellite
to say Pardon, Pardon, the two of us leaping
from one hope to another, carefully,
as if something might break in the process,
a constant static washing over every word
and hesitation, like a rain to make the dry leaves
slouch on their branches and snails revive beneath,
and holy mother of all, I said, or thought,
is the long summer finally over, and by the time
you answered, the true rain was already pelting
against both our windows, its patter there
and on the line finally making our voices softer.

Ferry

Ours was the last of the cars to squeeze onto the ferry,
all our prayers directed to the controllers of traffic
finally answered. Yes, we were blessed.

On the car radio that long day, those who delighted
in promoting our guilt had spoken of God become flesh,
more precisely, of a deity in diapers, an image
that seemed to touch on the reasons for our travel:
family, the habitual Christmas. Deity in diapers —
wow! This theology we thought we could live with!

Granny had laid her corsage with its braids of tinsel
and arabesques of green spray-paint on the back seat
beside her and complained she was tired. No wonder,
all of us talking nonstop and everyone on the radio
talking nonstop and mostly nonsense at that.

A few days before, she complained, at the shrink's,
she had failed all the tests that had had her spell
words backwards, retrace geometric shapes backwards,
count backwards from 100 by sevens or eights.
Every one of the clocks she'd been asked to draw
came out totally wrong, their numbers all bunched
together in a low corner or off to one side.

We tried to console her, trying at the same time
to hide our own anxieties over how long it took us
to spell 'world,' for example, backwards, to count
past 93, 86, 79…. We said, how can doing anything
backwards be a sign of either failure or success?

Unconvinced, she refused later to join in our game
of naming the relatives waiting for us across the strait,
game that our kids quickly won. She kept looking at them,
at us, then down at the grey water as the ferry slowly
took us across, the muscles of her face twitching,
as if there were something important she had to remember

Torschluss *

The air flickers and rises, everything in it.
Breathe it in.
Breathe out.
Let it go.
Stop brooding about how it works on others,
hikers and bikers this first day of summer.
Forget them.
Focus instead on crickets in the bush,
in the rising broom, clicking,
or on the broom's thick blossoming,
its dark pods that spiral open, catapulting
black seeds outward, too quick for the eye,
slow enough for earth and ear.
And the woman ahead, shadowed
by a younger man hot on her trail,
who may or may not remind you of yourself –
if you cannot say what you're after,
take a moment to gather your thoughts.
Consider each of the distinctions between
the woman, her shadow, and you.
Who cares if she rides her bike slowly,
giving and taking her own sweet time?
Don't even begin to pretend it's for you.
Wipe the sweat from your eye.
Lick the salt from your lip.

———————

* Literally: shutting of the gates. Closing time.
Torschlusspanik is the fear of older people that
they won't achieve their goals or find a spouse.

Let her pedal, backpedal, brake, then push
her bike at less than the young man's speed,
ratchets clicking, tacking into and
out of your line of vision –
no help now from impossible Zeno!
Is *that* what you're thinking?
Let it go.
She's easy to dismiss; shake him off too.
And don't imagine her elsewhere, dangling
first one foot, then the other,
into lake or bath water.
Turn your back on her and your own image
of her meticulously pumiced foot
sliding evenings into its shoe or glass slipper
clacking up the long wood of your staircase
come morning, breaking into your sleep,
kicking through sunlight that angles past
your bedroom window.
Don't believe these promises of heat and light
even if they make you feel decades younger.
Watch out for the easy miracles, stiletto heels
on which your fancy's too gladly impaled.
Let the woman and the man make their own way.
Go halfway home.
Then half of that.
And another half and half again.
And if this way you reach your door,
lock it behind you.
Set the chain.

Kingdoms of Absence

Relying on the old maps, they travel
through a country that no longer exists
to take pictures of a wall
that no longer stands.

They drive slowly and keep
their impressions to themselves.

So long as they do not try to sell it,
everything they carry with them
rises in value, whatever they find,
whatever they buy or are given.

No one in the towers records their progress
on the still functional roads.

Surveillance cameras on top of buildings
in the public squares have all,
they assume, been disconnected.

Hidden microphones are another matter,
and the natives who listen
and swallow their answers.

No one can say with any precision
from which direction the electricity flows.

They have names for the wind,
but nothing much to protect against it.
They have a few trees.

They see the noxious clouds shift
east to west, west to east
and back again.

So they still have east.
So they still have west.

Puppets

Because of you, master, the early bird's early,
the night owl late. One finds its worm, the other
its darkness. On your strings, all the golden corn
for which we hunger strains sunward. Deeper into earth
you force the edible and the inedible tubers.
When you shake a fist, all the clouds press against
a silver lining with which you hold our attention.
They burst over our fields and, though the thunder
startles us no longer, you see to it that we cower
and tremble. You make the moon wax and wane and keep
to cycles of which we do not long to be free.
When your mood swings, you shift the constellations
around, those stars on which we've pinned our hopes,
thinking they come from you. The borders need
constant adjusting. On them, you have us raise
ever higher walls. When you relent or grow bored,
you allow the guards to nod off, so that we fall
briefly out of their sights and begin running
in all the directions. With a snap of your fingers,
with one shot, you bring us back to our senses.
Will the razor wire ever be rolled up again?
One day, you have the Chinese students dancing
in their squares, then it's the European dance
in which shadows of soldiers guarding your memorials
still goosestep like the shadows of those soldiers
you've had them defeat. Even as you speak of the sun,
you turn to the night, its electricity. It's rumoured
that you understand computers. However we resist
speaking your name, it enters into all our prayers.
It's whispered in each of our curses. Whether we pray

or curse, you smile at us, as if nothing mattered
but that we pay attention. Someday, you tell us,
and we repeat your words often, we'll be free
of each other. Is it in our dream or yours that,
with emaciated arms, we wave you on your way?

III.

Two Blues

1. that particular blue into which
   at a thought
   all thoughts disappear

   and a breeze to scatter it
   and them

   along the shore
   whatever's straw and not straw
   easing sunward

   and a weak urge to grasp
   what's offered here

   blue of sky against blue of water
   and what lies behind

   as along the edge
   where they seem to meet
   a ship steams away smaller
   and smaller

   its passengers gazing at the wake
   luckier   less and less
   self-conscious

2. into the blue of ocean and beyond

into a lighter blue mist
on its far shore and higher

into the paler blue of mountains
rising from the mist
and up the blue glaciers on them

into reflections
and a white that finally caps them

through snow ice and clouds

vanishing into them as into a water
of which most of the body is made

Flies: A Few Questions

1. These flies on a white table burst
into shafts of light and touch down
again, sun-stricken,
the oil of their bodies breaking
light into all its parts.

   Not yet song, their buzzing proves
less than noise, maybe more,
horizon note or beginnings
of pattern.

   It suits me to think they have learned
to make much of the nothing
their lives amount to.

   What are you thinking?

2. We wake to the neighbourhood dogs
   and no wind.

   Two flies natter over the table.
   Still? Nothing sweeps them away
   and their sound.

   Top-heavy with their eyes,
   they return, circle and land,
   circle and land on the table.

   The dogs bark without letting up.

   How good a day can this be
   for ambitions?

3. Still the flies, furious, gleaming.

    How describe their sexless bodies,
    the transparency of their wings,
    their eyes, their eyes?

    Still the flies appear to us
    day and night and we fall
    into and out of dreams
    we will later insist
    we cannot live without.

    You draw the sheet higher,
    as if to protect us,
    but from what?

miniature: heliotropic

these rhodos
colossal

red echoes
of themselves

each sound (bronze
bee inside)

each blossom
trumpeting

(be inside)
lending shape

and colour
to the appeal

A cat ambiguously

cries in the bushes, in the woods
behind our house, voices what we think
fear or pain or feline equivalent for love,
those abstractions for which we have
not yet devised successful metaphors.
We need to approach them catlike, tentative,
with each of our lives, or turn instead
to the late afternoon or the night again,
familiar high sun or low moon cutting
the woods apart, marking its oaks and its broom
with shadows in which a cat, hunting
for what we can only guess, tries to lose
its shadow and likely does not find it
peculiar. The air, then, assumes
the almost timeless guise of our room,
venetian blinds slicing the sun or moon,
like the trees cut by the light in turn,
into discrete pieces. In sleep you struggle
to come up with fitting sounds for this.
Your mouth goes through its waking motions,
responding it seems by instinct to each
of the various appeals from outside.

Sultry Weather

The shoreline has been tied together
loosely and with thinnest string.
Sunbathers both male and female
are weighed down by mounds of sand,
paperweights, and ponderous,
inappropriate costume jewellery.
Dandelions strain against their roots,
as do the refugees. Even the woman
from a Victorian Age hikes up
her heavy skirts and lets them pull
her hands down again. Chinese sunhats
will not come off in this wind, though
they shift from one side of the brain
to the other, making more difference
than you might think. Words catch
on air and tangle into long phrases,
the phrases themselves tangling
on one another. More and more,
I anticipate whatever you are going
to say and say it myself. The air
has never felt so thin and,
when the mood threatens to slip,
I need only pull you in.

Narcissus

The sun does not get its act together,
nor cloud nor rain nor wind,
everything becalmed but the observer,
untouched by smooth water
on which sailboats do not sail.

Deadheads do not break through
the surface, on which a thin cloud cover
or thick haze weighs like oil.

What bits of light penetrate
give the water a grey sheen in which
boulders, washed for years from the cliff,
might, if they used all their senses,
recognize a part of themselves.

A barge full of coal or shavings loses
its contours, as does the inaudible tug,
almost invisible now.

The inaudible tug!

Mountains often observed in the distance
are lost for the duration to haze,
motors here and there kicking in,
as if the haze could be cheated,
as if goals could be had, ambitions.

Gulls close to shore, children
seen *and* heard, drop clams onto rocks,
mussels, crabs, their hunger defined,

therefore satiable.

Starlings One August

On the neighbourhood roofs, homeless starlings
frightened from one part of the city to another
by their own cries of distress, recorded and played
back later at random intervals, finished off
the red plums, picked them not quite clean
and dropped them to the asphalt. What blackness!
It seemed a perfect day for cursing politicians
and the slavish workers who executed their decisions,
not to mention dimwit Europeans who had brought
the birds here in the first place to maintain
their ties to the homeland, their needs and odd
cultural assumptions. Soon, the misfit birds
would be dropping pits and dark red pulp
all over Victoria, making unnatural enemies
of everyone. Shitting, breeding, stealing fruit,
squawking, taking up space, bullying songbirds aside –
what good did they do? The first confused reports
of looting and rape were coming out of Kuwait,
only days ago annexed by Saddam Hussein. Sad-faced
neighbours listened, watched unripe plums torn
from branches along with the ripe ones and flung
to the roofs and driveways below. They turned
their radios and TVs up full volume, clapped
their hands, exploded paper bags, shouted, threw
pens, pencils, ice cubes – whatever lay handy.
Ignoring the bylaws, they fired 22s and 10-
and 12-gauge shotguns into the busy air, but nothing
could stop the constant *flup flup* of the birds
or their chatter on the roofs and in the plum trees,
flup, flup, very haikuish, though far more insistent,

77

far less deliberate, offering only ongoing noise,
with no silence after to accommodate illumination.
This and everything else about them, their gibberish,
their disdain for those who would drive them off,
their oiliness some found beautiful – all of it
made the blood suddenly boil. Because of them,
somehow, it seemed possible, even probable,
that the West would never manage to solve the puzzle
of the Middle East, the nomadic Arabs never take
their place beside the wandering Jews, and Christians
under house arrest in Baghdad, Basra and Al Kuwait
never return to their homes, nor those sheiks
who found themselves abused by skinheads in London,
Paris and Berlin. And even though all Fairfield
cursed them and tried to force them to scatter,
the starlings kept up a constant noise, making
a bigger and bigger mess of everything.

Sombre

a cat on the fence
just high enough

out of the snow
on which the birdseed
lies scattered

in this light black
and likely
thinking black

and the clouds
in the background
sure enough darkening

Cappucine Order

In the gap between lamentation and praise,
leaves spin down in their colours and the moss
thickens into green. Ferns passive all summer
all raise their fronds at once. Somewhere behind
sight and sound, beside it: what a better eye
or ear might take in, a hummingbird's or bee's,
stilling the human pulse. It's no exact science,
this relentless gauging of the self's small part
in the passage, cells acting on their codes
or only giving in to them, some tired
of sun and photosynthesis, while others
go about their work, mitosis or meiosis
or only miracle, as if such process could
never stop. Flickers face off by the water,
less intent all at once on what the bark
of oaks may hold than on each other: bobbing
and singing their small repeated note, they break
the flock down into pairs. What the heart does
with this seems to depend on how long it's beaten.
Between bare rock and air, a new fungus grows.
What was hard proves soft again, and easier.

Sea Lion

The gulls are in a flap again,
as though the dead flesh further down
the shore would not suffice.

Another sea lion has become entangled
in the lines of a drift net and drowned.

For a week now, the stink has risen
and spread into town, the gulls
raising their own.

Dogs unleashed go after them, howling,
until the gulls bark back,
having no bite,

and fly off, squawking, shitting,
returning again and again.

These bits of evidence keep mounting
until the argument can no longer
be resisted.

We have sifted through everything
and weighed it, have tried
to keep our dogs chained.

We've kicked up our own ruckus
to chase off the birds, always
too hungry, or stubborn, or stupid
to let the corpse go.

This Morning, Hanging by a Thread

Spiders shook in their webs, caterpillars
inside their tents. They hung on threads, heading
slowly earthward from them. The sun appeared
as if created for nothing but to show off
the monarch's wing. Moonlight, then,
just for moths? we wondered. At breakfast,
the wasps seemed stickier than usual, confused
or irritated by our presence, maybe groggy like us
in the heat. Carnivores, they ignored butter and jam,
conspicuously, and went straight for the meat,
all too attached to its sinew and fat. How seldom,
you said, do we think things through to the end.
The insects made us think again, follow their thread
right down to the ground, down to soil and grass
where lowly crane flies first begin to err
through the brief inevitability of their lives,
unthinking, thinking neither happy nor unhappy.

Solar Machine

It's oiled and ready to go, and its skin hums
with near perfection, all the bones firing in synch.

It floats in the same saline water that supports
what you desire, drifts back to shore again,
against some flesh-coloured log or rock,
there applies its lotions, its greases and screens.

Smoke rising over the city keeps its distance,
as do the workers who live there, with no choice
but to breathe it in and breathe it out again, reflex
that gives them no larger share of the sacred.

The morning glory roars and shifts into lowest gear,
grinds up cliffs that define the beach,
while wasps cruise alongside, practically coasting.

You do not say No and cannot say Yes.

Other bodies race along also, double-clutching,
impressive, though nothing can put up a real challenge
to the sun with its superior engine.

And you hear the crickets finally run out of gas,
or do not hear it.

No sooner do the waves of this silence wash over them,
than the male and female swimmers stop struggling:
they sink once, twice and a third time.

When they surface again, your ears are ringing
with a significant history.

It gives a low whistle, while others near the shore
turn on emergency generators and sputter back
into one another's arms.

You bet it's electric.

Wintry Light

Snow catches awhile in poplars
that angle into clouds over the sun:

tricks of light in this season
given meaning by light
and the idea of light.

What other things does it have
up its sleeve, the season, that is,
and the idea also?

Candles?
Flames of poplars in September,
as memory prefers them?

They gutter out of modified versions
of the past and back again,
light and wax reinvented,

while the idea of snow covers
the idea of leaves beneath the poplars,
everything cumulative, even this.

Little Spring Songs

1.   Winter stops biting hard and deep,
   the spring not yet sure where to set
   its teeth, leaving us
   these bad metaphors, the seasonal jazz –
   wind instruments, puffs
   of nothing much that determines
   the music.

   The going eases as we go:
   otherwise, how could we contain all
   this who knows how to say or sing
   what's inside us, jawbone shattering,
   chattering right into summer?

   Not to mention put words to it:
   erotics of spring,
   the little green erections,
   green nudge, green wink,
   grass stains at the knee?

2. First love, first shame,
   first fear of expulsion
   by the parent-god who forgets
   to leave the porch light on.

   These are memories, too,
   not just metaphor, as Mandelstam
   would have it, that the world is full of,
   casting their green light
   always back on the world,

   words that direct us back
   to the grasses,
   the grasses themselves pointing
   to all the kept and unkept promises
   of their green
   and what that amounts to:

   pastures, psalms, a joyous singing.

3. What's to explain? Spring
   has arrived and brought
   none of its cruelties. We talk
   long into evening and keep
   the sun on our skins. Yes,
   we could call it habit
   or pattern and live with that.
   Last fall's horse apples
   have built a good soil,
   and the late winter's made
   little difference: tulips, irides,
   roses have survived and are thriving.
   What was the question? The Arab
   gelding's shedding his white coat
   like a cat's. Why do I mention
   cats when we don't have them?
   You could probably answer that;
   it's not a trick question.
   Or urge me outside again (who,
   now, is urging whom?) to watch
   the sun burn the dew away
   from the simple grass that covers
   all the black soil and does so
   without taking up much room.

Acknowledgements

Thanks to the editors of the following periodicals for first publishing poems in this collection: *Arc, And Yet, The Antigonish Review, Black Apple, B.C. Books, Canadian Fiction Magazine, Canadian Literature, Dalhousie Review, The Fiddlehead, Grain, The Malahat Review, Matrix, Prairie Fire, Prism international* and *Quarry*.

A version of 'One Version of Love' appeared in *The MacMillan Anthology 1*, edited by John Metcalf and Leon Rooke.

'Decent Neighbourhood', 'Night Rain', 'Keeping Up Appearances', 'In Autumn', 'Head', 'Two Blues', 'miniature: heliotropic', 'A cat ambiguously' and 'Angel in the House and Out' appeared in a chapbook, *Door Slowly Closing*, published by the Hawthorne Society.

For the generous application of his scalpel and tuning fork, a special thanks to Don McKay.

About the Author

Though born in Germany and for the most part (45 / 53 to be precise) shaped on the West Coast of Canada, Derk Wynand has at various times felt homesick for Quebec, Portugal, France and Mexico. Since 1969, he has taught at the University of Victoria, where he currently chairs the Department of Writing and edits *The Malahat Review*.